GARETH STEVENS
VITAL SCIENCE
Physical Science

TRANSFER OF ENERGY

by Simon de Pinna
Science curriculum consultant: Suzy Gazlay, M.A.,
science curriculum resource teacher

Gareth Stevens
Publishing

Please visit our Web site at: www.garethstevens.com
For a free color catalog describing Gareth Stevens Publishing's
list of high-quality books and multimedia programs, call
1-800-542-2595 (USA) or 1-800-387-3178 (Canada).
Gareth Stevens Publishing's fax: 1-877-542-2596

Library of Congress Cataloging-in-Publication Data

Pinna, Simon de.
  Transfer of energy / Simon de Pinna.
    p. cm. — (Gareth stevens vital science. Physical science)
  Includes bibliographical references and index.
  ISBN–13: 978-0-8368-8091-5 (lib. bdg.)
  ISBN–13: 978-0-8368-8100-4 (softcover)
  1. Energy transfer. 2. Force and energy. I. Title.
QC73.P56   2006
531'.6—dc22   2006033733

This edition first published in 2007 by
Gareth Stevens Publishing
A Weekly Reader Company
1 Reader's Digest Rd.
Pleasantville, NY 10570-7000 USA

Produced by Discovery Books
Editors: Rebecca Hunter, Amy Bauman
Designer: Clare Nicholas
Photo researcher: Rachel Tisdale

Gareth Stevens editorial direction: Mark Sachner
Gareth Stevens editors: Carol Ryback and Gini Holland
Gareth Stevens art direction: Tammy West
Gareth Stevens graphic design: Dave Kowalski
Gareth Stevens production: Jessica Yanke and Robert Kraus

Illustrations by Stefan Chabluk
Photo credits: CFW Images: 5, 23, 38, 40 (Edward Parker/EASI-Images); 8 (Adrian Cooper/
EASI-Images); 30 (Chris Fairclough); CORBIS: 35; Corus/Newscast: 27; Getty Images:
18 (Pete Turner); 21 (David Fleetham); Istockphoto: Cover (Shaun Lowe); 4 (Greg Nicholas);
10 (Eric Foltz); 11 (Matthew Scherf); 12, title page (Matt Matthews); 14, 17 (Amy Goodchild);
22 (Kirk Strickland); 25 (Neal McClima, 28 (Wendy Nero); 31 (Ana Abejan); 32 (Thomas Mounsey);
33 (Rene Mansi); 34 (Andrew Green); 39 (Graham Prentice); 43 left, 43 right (Logan Buell);
Science Photo Library: p. 7 (Sovereign, ISM).

Printed in the United States of America

2 3 4 5 6 7 8 9 10 10 09 08

TABLE OF CONTENTS

Words that appear in the glossary are printed in **boldface** type the first time they appear in the text.

Cover: Fireworks on July 1st in Bedford, Nova Scotia, for Canada Day celebrations.

Title page: Hot bodies glow with infrared radiation. The hottest parts of the body appear yellow. Cooler areas are red, purple, or even blue.

Introduction

Energy is everywhere. It makes things move and takes many forms. When anything moves—a ball bounces or a child rides a bicycle—energy makes it "happen." When something changes—water is boiled to create steam or coal is burned to feed a fire—energy makes that happen, too.

What Is Energy?

Energy exists in many forms. Different kinds of energy make different things happen. Whenever one kind of energy makes something happen, it can even change into one—or sometimes more than one—of the other forms.

You get energy from the food you eat. Some **machines**, such as cars or stoves, get their energy from gasoline or natural gas. Like food, gasoline and natural gas are fuels. The energy locked inside them can be released so that the machine—or body—can do its work.

Have you heard someone say, "You've got lots of energy?" It probably means you're being very active. You can tell that you've "got energy" because of what you can do

with it—run, swim, or ride a bicycle. In fact, the more running around you do, the less energy you have left. You're like a tightly wound spring winding down. But after you rest and refuel (eat), you're full of energy again.

Food, such as meat, gives you all the energy you need to keep warm and move around.

Electromagnetic Spectrum

Light and heat energy travel in waves, as do other forms of energy, such as radio waves, infrared and ultraviolet waves, and microwaves. These waves are called electromagnetic waves because they are

ENERGY

"Energy and persistence alter all things."

Benjamin Franklin, American scientist and diplomat, (1706–90)

a combination of magnetic and **electrical energy**. The main difference between the various forms of **electromagnetic radiation** is their wavelength—the distance from the top, or crest, of one wave to the crest of the next. All electromagnetic waves have a different frequency—the number of waves per second. There's a connection: the longer the wavelength, the lower the frequency.

The **electromagnetic spectrum** shows the range of electromagnetic waves from the longest to the shortest. The longest waves, radio waves, tend to spread out as they travel, which makes them useful for broadcasting. These waves are sent by

transmitters and carry signals to your radio or television. Radio waves are also given off by stars, lightning, and sparks. That's why you sometimes get **interference** on your radio during a thunderstorm.

Microwaves are produced by different kinds of transmitters. They are also given off by stars. Microwaves cook certain foods by causing water and fat **molecules** to vibrate, which heats substances containing those molecules. Microwaves are also used in broadcasting, radar, and wireless technology. Your cell phone has a microwave chip and antenna, but it is so small that it needs to be within reach

For many people, wind energy has been an important part of daily life for centuries.

of a system of transmitter towers to send your call very far.

There are two types of infrared (IR) waves. Those with comparatively shorter wavelengths carry heat from the Sun. Other heat sources, such as a heater or radiator, give off longer infrared waves. In fact, everything that is warm gives off IR waves—including you. IR waves have many uses, including the TV remote, security motion detectors, and satellite photos used for weather forecasting. Some night vision goggles use infrared waves to detect differences in **temperature** between objects and their surroundings. An infrared camera uses IR rays instead of light to take pictures. The results—called thermograms-—show different temperatures in different colors.

Visible light waves are the only electromagnetic waves humans can see. While we do not see actual waves, we perceive the energy they carry as different colors. Each color has a different wavelength—from red, the longest, to violet, the shortest. These waves combine to make white light.

Ultraviolet (UV) waves are shorter than visible light waves. We can't see ultraviolet light, but some insects can. The Sun gives off massive amounts of UV light. This part of sunlight tans (and sometimes burns) our skin. Reasonable exposure to UV light

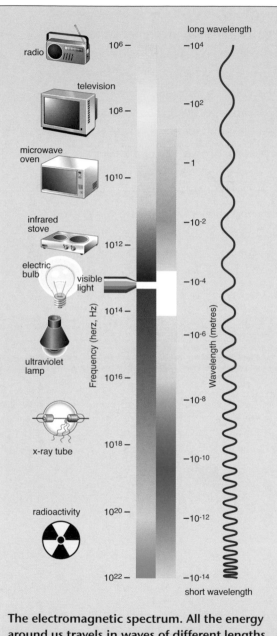

The electromagnetic spectrum. All the energy around us travels in waves of different lengths, from gamma rays at short wavelengths through the visible spectrum of light to the longest radio waves.

causes our bodies to produce Vitamin D. UV rays can be used to kill **microbes** and sterilize equipment.

The electromagnetic waves with the shortest wavelengths and the highest frequencies have the most energy, so they are the most powerful. X-rays can pass through most materials, which makes them useful to see inside things such as our bodies or luggage at the airport. Lower-energy X-rays can be used to scan softer areas, such as the digestive system or brain.

Gamma rays are given off by stars and radioactive materials. These powerful rays can go through just about any material except thick concrete or lead. They can kill living cells, which is good if they are directed at cancer cells. Gamma rays are also used to kill microbes and sterilize equipment and food.

Tracers

Several life-threatening medical conditions, such as heart disease and bone cancer, can be detected using radioactive molecules that give off gamma rays. This detection is possible because some chemical elements concentrate in certain parts of the body, such as iodine in the thyroid, phosphorus in the bones, and potassium in muscles. When a patient is injected with a radioactive version of any of those elements, called tracers, a special camera that is sensitive to gamma rays (given off by the radioactive **atoms**) can take sequences of pictures, which look almost like movies, to reveal whether the organs are working properly or not.

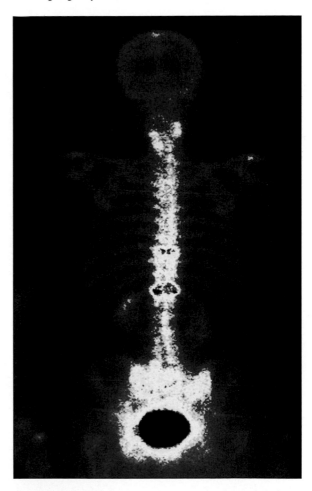

This photograph shows the spine of a 68-year-old person who has been damaged by osteoporosis. The patient has been injected with a radioactive tracer that accumulates in the damaged bones. A gamma camera is then used to detect the gamma rays emitted by the tracer, shown here in red.

CHAPTER 1

Heat

Everything has heat energy, whether you call it "hot" or "cold." The difference is that a cup of hot water, for example, has more heat energy than the same amount of cold water. We put heat energy to good use when we cook our food or burn fuel to keep our homes warm.

NO SMOKE WITHOUT FIRE

"The best way to make a fire with two sticks is to make sure one of them is a match."

Will Rogers, American entertainer, 1879–1935

Fire is a source of both heat and light energy, as is shown by these street vendors in the city of Kaili, in China.

Heat and Temperature

Heat is not the same as temperature. A spoonful of boiling water could be at the same temperature as a pan of boiling water, but the pan of water contains more heat energy than the water in the spoon.

If you look closely at the spoon—or any other substance—under a powerful microscope, you will see that it is made of tiny vibrating particles—atoms and molecules. The faster the particles vibrate, the more heat energy is present. When you use a thermometer to measure the temperature of something, you are measuring the average amount of energy in the particles surrounding the end of the thermometer.

Moving Heat

Heat energy naturally flows from an object or area of higher temperature to an object

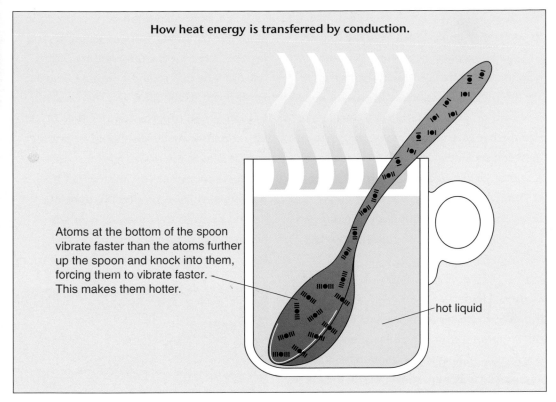

How heat energy is transferred by conduction.

Atoms at the bottom of the spoon vibrate faster than the atoms further up the spoon and knock into them, forcing them to vibrate faster. This makes them hotter.

hot liquid

or area of lower temperature. It can travel in three different ways: **conduction**, **convection**, or **radiation**.

Conduction

If you use that powerful microscope again to look at a cold spoon in a hot drink, you will see that the molecules of the hot drink are vibrating rapidly against the outer molecules of the cold spoon and passing along some of their energy. Then those spoon molecules begin to vibrate faster and knock against the molecules next to them, causing them to vibrate faster, too, and so on, all the way to the end of the spoon's handle. When all molecules in both drink and spoon are vibrating at the same frequency, the drink and spoon will be the same temperature—in a sort of balance called equilibrium. This movement of heat energy from molecule to molecule is called conduction.

Metals are generally good conductors because heat moves quickly from atom to atom inside them. Objects made from other materials usually conduct heat less well because their molecules do not pass on their energy as easily. A material that slows down or blocks the movement of heat energy is called an insulator. One such material,

Transfer of Energy

fiberglass, is often used to insulate homes. Its molecules don't pass on energy quickly.

Liquids, such as water, don't conduct heat as well as metals. Gases, such as air, are the poorest conductors of all. Gas molecules are so far apart compared to solids or liquids that very little heat energy is passed between molecules. Air is a good insulator. A winter jacket made of materials with lots of surface area, such as acrylic or down fibers, traps air near your body. The trapped air slows the loss of your body heat, which keeps you warm.

Convection

If there is a heater on in a room, it will heat the air around it. As the air becomes warmer, its molecules become more active and move farther apart. As a result, the air becomes less dense, so it rises. As it goes up over the heater, gravity causes the cooler (denser) air to move down and take its place. As the hot air moves farther away from the heater, it cools, becomes more dense again, and starts to sink. In this way, a flow or current of air circulates around the room while the heater is on. This way of moving heat energy, where hot particles rise above cooler ones because they are lighter, is called convection. The circular flow of warmer and cooler air is called a convection current.

Convection is the most common way for heat to travel through gases and liquids, because those molecules are free to move.

You may be able to observe convection in action all around you. For example, you may be able to feel a temperature difference in a heated room by putting your hand down to the floor and then reaching as high as you can. The temperature in the upper part of the room should be warmer than it is near the floor. That's a room-sized convection current you are feeling! If, on a cold winter day, you open the door of a heated room to the outdoors, you will begin a convection current on a much larger scale. The warmer air inside the room

Birds are masters of gliding on thermals — the heat convection air currents that rise up over the land as it warms.

will immediately begin to flow out the door and rise into the cooler air outside.

Convection plays an important part in the natural world. Early in the day, heat radiated from the Sun starts warming the Earth's surface. The ground then heats the cooler air above it by convection. As the air gets warmer, it expands and rises, and cooler air moves in to take its place. Just as happened in the heated room, a convection current is created, but this time it's on a much larger scale. Convection currents resulting from uneven heating of the Earth's surface are the cause of winds, from the smallest breezes to the most violent tornado. These currents are responsible for atmospheric circulation around the globe!

In the oceans, sun-warmed water from the equator region moves north and south toward colder water. The resulting convection current forms warm-water currents such as the **Gulf Stream** in the Atlantic Ocean. Convection is also taking place deep

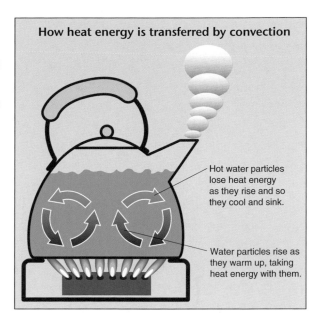

How heat energy is transferred by convection

Hot water particles lose heat energy as they rise and so they cool and sink.

Water particles rise as they warm up, taking heat energy with them.

JAMES DEWAR (1842–1923)

James Dewar was a chemist, physicist, and the inventor of the thermos flask. Born in Scotland, Dewar was a professor of chemistry at the University of Cambridge and a member of the Royal Institution of Great Britain.

Among his scientific discoveries, Dewar constructed a machine for producing liquid oxygen. He invented the Dewar, or vacuum flask (later known as the thermos flask), in 1892.

The vacuum flask is a container for storing hot or cold substances, especially the very cold liquid gases with which Dewar worked. This container consists of two flasks. One is inside the other; the two are separated by a vacuum. The vacuum cuts down the movement of heat by conduction, so it slows temperature changes.

The walls of the inner flask were originally made of glass because glass is a poor conductor of heat. The flask's surfaces were covered with silver, a shiny metal that reflects any infrared radiation back into the contents and so reduces the transfer of heat by radiation.

within our planet. In the **mantle**, **magma** near the Earth's core is hotter than the magma closer to the surface. The hot magma rises and then cools and sinks, pushing warmer magma to the top of the mantle.

Another example of convection in nature is a rising column of warm air called a thermal. Thermals often develop in areas where one part of the ground is warmer than the ground surrounding it. You can often see birds, wings outstretched, riding the thermals on a hot day. With skill, birds can travel by moving from one thermal to another before the air cools and they have to descend.

Radiation

Heat radiation—also called infrared radiation—is the form of heat energy that can travel through the vacuum of outer space as an electromagnetic wave. It is part of the spectrum of electromagnetic radiation produced by the Sun and absorbed by the Earth. Our skin absorbs infrared radiation readily, enabling us to feel the heat of a fire without having to touch it.

As is true with conduction and convection, radiated heat moves from hotter objects to cooler ones. The hotter the object, the more heat radiation it sends out. If you stand in front of a heater, you will get warmer, not only because of convection but also because your body is absorbing infrared waves.

Some surfaces are better at absorbing heat radiation than others. If you wear a

Hot bodies glow with infrared radiation. The hottest parts of the body appear yellow — cooler areas are red, purple or even bluc.

white T-shirt on a sunny day, you won't feel as hot as if you had worn a black T-shirt. This is because black surfaces absorb infrared radiation better than white surfaces. White and shiny surfaces are very good at reflecting heat radiation, just as **mirrors** are good at reflecting light rays. That's why satellites are covered in shiny foil. The foil reflects the Sun's infrared radiation and prevents sensitive electronic components in the satellite from getting too hot.

Did You Know?

HOW HOT?
People have different ideas of what feels hot and what feels cold. Scientists use several different numbers to describe the "hotness" of an object. These are all measures of what we call temperature.

You might know two of these temperature scales. One, the Celsius scale, was invented by Swedish astronomer Anders Celsius. Another, the Fahrenheit scale, was invented by Polish-born German physicist Gabriel Fahrenheit. So the temperature can be given in "degrees Celsius" or "degrees Fahrenheit." For example, water boils at 100 degrees Celsius (written as 100 °C) or 212 degrees Fahrenheit (212 °F).

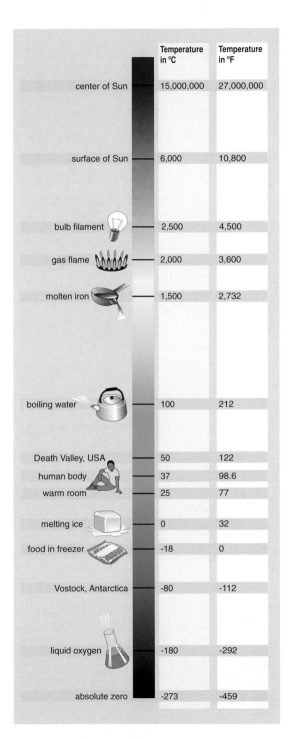

	Temperature in °C	Temperature in °F
center of Sun	15,000,000	27,000,000
surface of Sun	6,000	10,800
bulb filament	2,500	4,500
gas flame	2,000	3,600
molten iron	1,500	2,732
boiling water	100	212
Death Valley, USA	50	122
human body	37	98.6
warm room	25	77
melting ice	0	32
food in freezer	-18	0
Vostock, Antarctica	-80	-112
liquid oxygen	-180	-292
absolute zero	-273	-459

CHAPTER 2

Light

Light is a form of energy we use every day. Stars such as the Sun are constantly changing the energy of their atoms into light and heat energy, which travel as electromagnetic waves and reach us through space. Just by standing in the sunlight, you can feel the energy that it carries. It can heat up your body and even burn your skin. There's enough energy in the light falling on a square yard (.836 square meter) of the Earth to power ten 100-watt electric lightbulbs!

Light Energy

Without **light energy**, we wouldn't be able to see anything. An object becomes visible only when light from the Sun or another source of light, such as a flashlight, bounces off the object and enters our eyes.

Like other electromagnetic waves, light transfers energy from one place to another. When light waves hit an object or surface, some of the energy they carry is transferred to the atoms in that material while some is reflected back. Those atoms that absorb light energy can change some of it into heat, causing the material to become warmer. Some atoms can also absorb light energy and send out new light waves of their own.

Light rays travel in straight lines away from a source of light. When they hit matter, there are several things that can happen. They can pass through the matter, they can be absorbed by it, or they can be reflected. When they pass through material, they can also be refracted, or bent.

Light rays travel in straight lines, so any object that blocks the light will look dark, like a shadow. That is what makes some clouds appear darker than others.

Absorption

Have you noticed that, on a sunny day, the dark asphalt gets hotter than the lighter cement curb or sidewalk nearby? Both are in the direct path of the Sun's energy, but the asphalt absorbs more light energy. Some of that energy is transferred to the asphalt molecules, causing the pavement to get warmer. Once again, how much energy is absorbed depends upon the type of material and the type of light wave striking it. The asphalt appears to be black because it is absorbing nearly all of the light falling on it and reflecting very little.

Transmission

When you look out the window, you can see whatever is on the other side even though there is glass in between. That's because some of the light waves that are reflected from those objects travel right through the glass and into your eyes. **Transmission** takes place when light waves hit a material and continue on through. How much light is transmitted depends upon the material and the type of light waves.

Reflection

When light waves hit a surface, whatever light energy is not transmitted or absorbed is reflected. The direction that the light is reflected depends upon the direction at which the incoming ray hit the surface. So, for example, if a single light ray strikes the surface from a 27° angle, it will be reflected away from the surface at the same angle, 27°, but in the opposite direction. Most likely, a large number of light rays are

LETTING LIGHT THROUGH?

Different materials absorb, transmit, and reflect light in different ways. **Transparent** materials, such as clear glass, let almost all light pass through. **Translucent** materials, such as frosted glass, let some light through, but not so much that you can see through it. **Opaque** materials, such as a brick wall, do not allow any light to pass through. That's why a solid (opaque) object makes a shadow if it's in the way of the light. The rays are blocked so you see a dark area on the side not reached by the light.

striking the surface at the same time, but each ray is acting on its own. If you could look closely at most surfaces, you would see that they are not absolutely flat. The incoming rays hit at slightly different angles, and the reflected rays are scattered in slightly different directions.

What happens when light hits a smooth or nearly smooth surface, especially one that is shiny? Unless it is a source of light, any object will reflect some light. Mirrors, however, are designed to reflect back nearly all the light that hits them. When you look at yourself in a flat ("plane") mirror, the picture you see of yourself—your image—appears to be as far behind the mirror as you are in front of it. Your brain is fooled into thinking that the light rays have traveled from an object behind the glass, but it is actually light reflected from the mirror that you see.

Not all mirrors are flat; some are curved. One, called a concave mirror, curves inward like a dish. This kind of mirror is sometimes used for shaving, so you may have seen one at home. If you look at yourself close up in a concave mirror, your image in the mirror will seem bigger than real life. You've been magnified! This is because the directions that the light rays take when they are reflected fools your brain into thinking you're much closer to the mirror than you are.

As you move away from the mirror, the image blurs; a bit farther away and you will

How an image forms in a plane mirror. The dotted lines show where the reflected light rays seem to come from.

mirror

image

light rays

see yourself small and upside down! This time, the reflected light rays have crossed over before they reach your eyes. This makes your brain think you're standing on your head!

Another type of curved mirror does just the opposite. Convex mirrors curve outward and give a wider view than a flat mirror. They are often used as a side-view mirror on the passenger side of a car. If you look at yourself in a convex mirror—or the back of a large spoon—the image you'll see of yourself will look right side up, but it will seem to be a long way away. That's why that side-view mirror may warn that objects reflected are closer than they appear.

All electromagnetic waves—including light—travel through space at a speed of about 186,000 miles/second (300,000 kilometers/second). No object or wave can move through the vacuum of empty space faster than this speed, which is called the speed of light.

Light waves slow down as they travel through matter, depending upon the density of the material and other factors. The molecules in air are so spread out that the speed of light traveling through air is only slightly less than its speed in space. In water, it drops significantly to about 140,000 miles (225,000 km) per second. The speed of light through clear glass is about 124,000 miles (200,000 km) per second because the glass, although transparent, is denser than water.

Refraction

When light rays moving through one material encounter a different material, they change direction. This change of direction is called **refraction**. Imagine, for example, a light ray hitting water in a glass bottle. The light bends when it starts going through the glass, and then it bends again when it starts going through the water. When the light ray encounters the wall of the glass again, it bends back a little. When it comes out of the glass and starts going through the air again, it bends back a little more. By this time, it has refracted, or changed direction, several times, because

A straight object standing in a liquid looks bent or enlarged because the light rays coming from it are refracted as they travel through the liquid.

it has encountered several different changes of materials.

You may have seen a prism—a solid piece of glass or transparent material that typically has a triangular base and rectangular sides (see page 18). A prism can be used to refract light in an unusual way. When a ray of light shines on a prism, the light bends once as it enters and once more as it leaves through the opposite side. If the light going into the prism is regular sunlight (called "white light"), then you can see that the light leaving the prism appears to be made of a number of colored rays, including red, orange, yellow, green, blue, indigo, and violet. The prism separates out the light waves according to their wavelengths. The red light waves are the longest and are bent the least. The violet waves, which are the shortest, are bent the most.

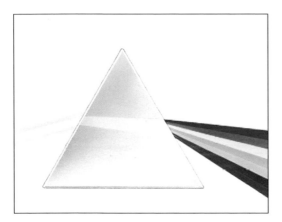

A prism bends the colors—or wavelengths—that make up sunlight by different amounts as a light ray passes through it. This means you can see the full spectrum from red to blue—just like a rainbow!

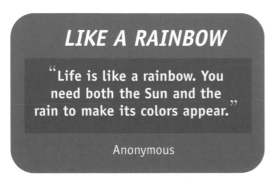

LIKE A RAINBOW

"Life is like a rainbow. You need both the Sun and the rain to make its colors appear."

Anonymous

Mirages

When light bends, we can be fooled by what we think we see. These tricks of the light are called mirages. The most common mirage is the appearance of water on a highway during a clear, hot day. Up ahead, you see what appears to be water on the highway. But when you reach the spot, the highway is dry!

Mirages are commonly seen in hot, dry places such as deserts. The shiny, shimmery patches on the asphalt look wet, but in fact they are produced by the Sun's rays being bent toward your eyes by the hot air just above the highway.

This mirage happens because light travels more quickly through hot air than through cooler air. The thin layer of hot air close to the ground bends the light rays coming from the sky along the road surface toward your eye. Your brain, assuming light always travels in a straight line, tries to make sense of the light from the bright sky, which now seems to be coming from the highway. So it sees a bright patch that it interprets as water!

Lenses

The fact that light bends when it passes from air into glass can work to our advantage. Specially shaped pieces of plastic or glass, called **lenses**, are purposefully used to bend light rays coming from an object. Depending on the type of lens used, the light rays are bent so as to meet at one point in front of the lens or appear to meet at a point behind the lens. Each of these

points is called the focal point of the lens. The distance from the center of the lens to the focal point is called the focal length.

A convex lens is thicker in the middle than at the edges. Light rays coming through the lens converge (come together) at a focal point on the other side of the lens from the object. This is where a clear image of the object can be seen or photographed. In fact, your eyes contain convex lenses. The muscles holding the lens in place adjust its shape to focus images on the light-sensitive cells at the back of your eye. A magnifying glass also has a convex lens—the thicker the lens, the greater the magnification.

A concave lens, on the other hand, is thinner at the middle than at the edges. Parallel light rays passing through a concave lens diverge, or spread out. Because the lens makes light rays spread out instead of bringing them together, the focus seems to be

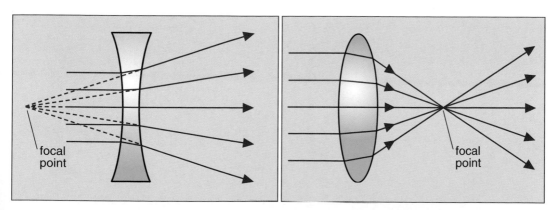

focal point

focal point

A concave lens *(left)* bends light rays so that they spread out. This makes a distant object appear closer than it really is. A convex lens *(right)* bends light rays so that they cross at the focal point of the lens. This is important if you're looking at something close to your eye.

behind the lens. This makes the object look smaller than it is.

Concave lenses can be very useful because they can help make details look clearer. They are often used together with convex lenses to help sharpen up any details that are lost because of errors with the convex lens. For example, concave lenses are fitted in glasses to help improve the eyesight of "nearsighted" people, who cannot see distant objects clearly.

How We See

Your eye is like a camera, with a lens to bend the light rays from an object to a focus at the back of the eye. There, the light forms an image on the retina, a thin layer of special light-sensitive cells. The retina is made up of two types of cells: rods and

cones. Rods simply detect light. Cones, however, respond to different colors in the light spectrum. Cones need brighter light to function than do the rods, which is why objects seem to lose their color at dusk or in dim light. Together, these cells send nerve messages to your brain, which puts the messages together to make an image of what you're seeing.

There are three types of cone cells, each one responding to different wavelengths of visible light. One responds to red and

How the human eye works. Light rays from objects we look at are bent by a flexible lens to form an image on a layer of light-sensitive cells, called the retina. These cells send signals along the optic nerve to the part of the brain that creates a picture of the world around us.

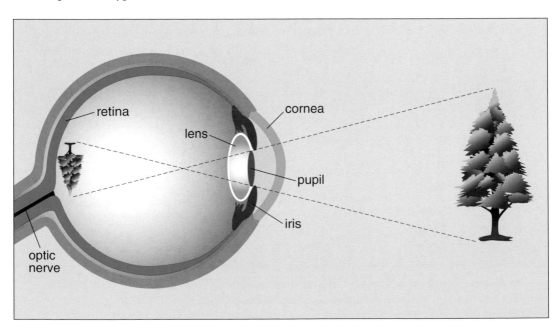

yellow waves, allowing you to see the color red; one responds to yellow and green waves, allowing you to see the color green; and one responds to blue and violet waves, allowing you to see the color blue. You might be wondering, what about the other colors? When light strikes your retina, the cones send signals to your brain. Your brain interprets these combinations as all the different colors that you are seeing.

BIOLUMINESCENCE

Bioluminescence is light produced by a chemical reaction inside a living thing. It is common in the deep ocean, where a quart (about a liter) of seawater can contain hundreds of single-celled algae—all producing a glowing light. On a larger scale, several meat-eating fish have luminous parts on their heads to attract curious prey.

Several underwater animals, such as this jellyfish, contain special bacteria that produce light. The jellyfish use the light to attract prey that they catch with their stinging tentacles.

Elsewhere in the ocean, certain squid and small crustaceans use clouds of bioluminescent chemicals in the same way as many squid use ink, to confuse or repel a predator while the squid or crustacean escapes to safety. Attracting a mate is another possible reason for bioluminescence. For example, fireflies (a type of beetle, also called lightning bugs) of both sexes flash their abdomens periodically to attract mates.

CHAPTER 3

Energy in Other Forms

Energy comes in many different forms, but each form belongs to one of two categories: kinetic (moving) energy or potential (stored) energy. One way to think of it is that kinetic energy is already happening, and potential energy is present and ready to go, but not yet active.

MUSIC AND MOVEMENT

"I conceived of an instrument that would create sound without using any mechanical energy, like the conductor of an orchestra. The orchestra plays mechanically, using mechanical energy; the conductor just moves his hands, and his movements have an effect on the music artistry."

Leon Theremin, Russian musician and inventor of the Theremin and electronic musical instruments, 1896–1993

Kinetic Energy

Anything that is moving has kinetic, or movement, energy. **Kinetic energy** is the motion found in atoms, molecules, and electrons. Waves have kinetic energy. So do any substances or objects that are moving. Moving water and wind are other examples. Kinetic energy is related to speed: The faster something is moving, the more kinetic energy it has. But, even when an object is not moving, all its particles—its atoms and molecules—are in random motion and thus have kinetic energy. For example, your soccer ball may be sitting absolutely still, but the air molecules inside it are in constant motion. Even though you can't see it, the molecules of the material from which the ball is made are moving too!

You give a ball movement or kinetic energy when you kick it.

Scientists can measure the amount of kinetic energy found in objects that are microscopically small as well as those that are unimaginably huge. Particles much smaller than molecules are hurtling through space and colliding with Earth all the time. Because the amount of kinetic energy in any moving object depends on both its size and its speed, these tremendously fast-moving particles have a lot more energy than you might think. Their energy can be measured using the scientists' sensitive instruments.

On a different scale, highly sensitive measuring devices are needed to record the vast amounts of kinetic energy released when rocks collide deep under the surface of the earth during an earthquake. This energy can travel all the way around the planet in the form of seismic waves.

Electrical Energy

Nearly everywhere you go, you can find electrical energy at work. This is a most useful form of kinetic energy because so many machines that make our lives easier (or more fun) use electrical energy to power them. Using electrical energy, electric fans keep us cool, televisions entertain us, cell

Cable cars need lots of electrical energy to carry people from the ground to the top of a mountain—and back again.

Transfer of Energy

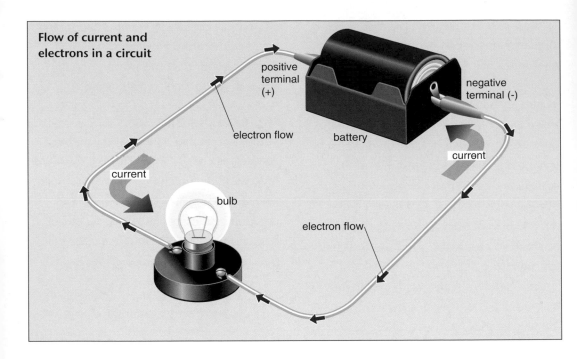

Flow of current and electrons in a circuit

positive terminal (+)

electron flow

battery

negative terminal (-)

current

current

bulb

electron flow

---

phones keep us in touch with each other, and light bulbs light our offices, schools, and homes after dark.

Electricity has a lot to do with electrons, the tiny particles that orbit around the nucleus of an atom. The electrons of some types of atoms can be made to move to a neighboring atom, setting up a **chain reaction** of electrons moving from one atom to the next. This movement creates an electrical current, or flow, as one electron attaches to a new atom, and another electron moves on. This flow is what is happening in the wires that carry electricity into and throughout your home. So, when you plug in a toaster, for example, electrical energy flows as a current from an outside source of electricity through wires into your

When you switch on a circuit, electrons flow from the negative terminal of the battery to the positive. At the same time, an electric current flows from the positive terminal to the negative.

house, then into a loop of wiring in the wall—a circuit—and then into the toaster.

Batteries, also known as cells, are portable sources of electrical energy. We use them to power flashlights, radios, cameras, cell phones, laptop computers, and many other machines. How many devices do you use that depend on the energy stored in batteries?

Batteries can be many shapes and sizes —from tiny, round batteries that fit into watches to huge ones that you couldn't begin to lift. They all have one thing in common: They contain substances that react when the battery is part of a circuit to change stored **chemical energy** into electrical energy.

But not all electrical energy is inside circuits made of wire. Think of the crackling noise you sometimes hear when you pull a sweater over your head in cold weather, and the tiny flashes of light you might see around the sweater if you pull it off in a darkened room. This is an example of what is often called static electricity, which is not actually static at all! The sparks happen when electrons (negative charges) jump from atoms on the surface of the sweater to your body.

On a bigger scale, lightning flashing across the sky is a giant electrical spark that leaps from the ground to a cloud. At the same time that it produces a very bright light, lightning also quickly heats the air, making the air expand so fast that it explodes, causing the sound of thunder.

Sound Energy

We live in a world full of sounds. Sounds can be as loud as a thunderous jet engine or as quiet as an ocean wave breaking quietly on the shore. Other sounds—such as a bird's song, a poet reciting a poem, or even a car's horn—have a purpose!

All these sounds, whether made naturally or by living things, are caused by vibrations. When an object vibrates, it moves from side to side rapidly. These movements make the surrounding air or water particles collide with each other and then move apart—over and over again.

If enough particles are moving backward and forward together, the energy will move from particle to particle when they collide, and that becomes a sound wave. The wave of energy moves out from the source of the sound and, if it is strong enough, will create a sound that reaches your ear. Although sound travels in the form of waves, sound waves are not part of the electromagnetic spectrum. Also, **sound energy** is a type of kinetic energy.

How does hearing take place? Your outer ear collects the sound waves, and your middle ear conducts them along to your inner ear. Your inner ear changes the sound waves into electrical impulses sent to your brain, and your brain interprets what you hear!

Birds depend on making the right sounds to identify themselves, attract mates, and defend their territories from competitors.

Transfer of Energy

Motion Energy

An object moves only if some sort of force is applied to it. That force might be a push or a pull, but without it, that object isn't going to budge. Motion energy is the kinetic energy involved in the movement of a substance or object from one place to another.

Radiant Energy

Energy that travels in the form of electromagnetic waves is called radiant energy. It, too, is a type of kinetic energy.

Potential Energy

Potential energy is another way of saying "stored energy." An object can have potential energy because of where it is, what it contains, or what's been done to it. One example would be a can of gasoline. It is stored energy, with the potential to release a lot of energy if it comes into contact with a match.

Gravitational Potential Energy

Think about what happens if you lift an apple above a table. You use your own stored energy to overcome the weight of the apple by moving it upward against gravity to a position above the table. Another way to say this is to say that you've overcome the force of gravity that kept the apple on the table. The higher you lift the apple, the more energy you use, and the more gravitational potential energy you have with respect to the table.

If you let go of the apple then, the potential energy stored in it as you lifted it is suddenly changed into kinetic energy as it falls toward the Earth. When the apple lands on the table, some of that kinetic energy then changes into sound energy ("thud!") and a bit of heat energy that raises the temperature of the apple and the surrounding air just a little. The rest is absorbed by the table and by the apple.

Other examples of gravitational potential energy include water stored in a reservoir behind a dam and a roller coaster pausing at the top of that first incline before it hurtles down the track.

Elastic Potential Energy

An elastic material can be stretched or squashed, but it will go back to its original size and shape if allowed to. Imagine a jack-in-the-box. The spring inside is squeezed, or compressed, by the lid when it's closed. The compressed spring has elastic potential energy, which is sometimes called stored mechanical energy. When you open the lid, the energy in the spring is changed into kinetic energy and the "jack" springs out.

The same elastic potential energy is stored in a rubber band when you stretch it. The piece of rubber contains potential energy when it is stretched, but that energy is changed into kinetic energy when you let go of one end. Think about what happens to a bungee cord the moment after it has

A roller coaster works because potential energy can be stored in the car when it goes up a slope against the pull of gravity, which is then changed to movement energy as the car accelerates down the track.

been stretched to the maximum by the weight and momentum of the falling jumper!

Chemical Energy

Chemical energy is a type of potential energy. It is the energy that is stored in bonds of atoms and molecules. In your body, chemical energy is stored in your muscles. Your muscles turn it into movement energy when you walk or run. When you get hot during a fast-moving game, that's because some of the chemical energy has been changed into heat energy by your muscles contracting and stretching as they pull on your bones and move your body.

Fuels are another type of chemical energy. We burn these to release their energy in the form of heat. Coal, oil, and gas—as well as many of the substances made from them, such as gasoline and kerosene—are all fuels. So are the logs we burn in our campfires or fireplaces. The carbohydrates, protein, and fat in the food we eat are fuels. Hydrogen is a fuel that may well power our cars in the near future.

When these fuels are burned, the energy locked in their molecules is changed rapidly into heat and light—think about the flames of a fire. We can use that heat energy to do useful things, such as heat a container of water until it becomes steam, which can have enough kinetic energy to turn the blades of a turbine to generate electricity. That's the basic idea behind most power plants.

Chemical energy in the food this baseball player eats is needed so that she can run from base to base!

Nuclear Energy

Nuclear energy is a form of potential energy stored in the center, or nucleus, of an atom. This energy can be released during a chain reaction known as a nuclear reaction.

Unlike the power plants that depend on coal, oil, or gas for the heat they need to turn liquid water into steam, in nuclear power plants the heat energy comes from splitting the atoms of certain elements, such as uranium. This process is called fission.

EINSTEIN'S ENERGY

"The release of atomic energy has not created a new problem. It has merely made more urgent the necessity of solving an existing one."

Albert Einstein, German American scientist, 1879–1955

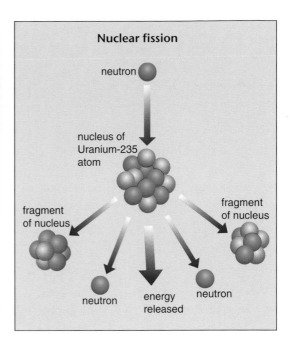

Nuclear fission

neutron

nucleus of Uranium-235 atom

fragment of nucleus

fragment of nucleus

neutron

energy released

neutron

Scientists use high-speed particles called neutrons to bombard the atoms of uranium until they split into smaller fragments. These fragments then collide with others and carry on what's known as a chain reaction. The term radioactive describes any atom that can be split into smaller atoms of different substances.

A fast-moving neutron collides with the nucleus of a uranium atom. It splits into two fragments, which then hit other atoms, setting up a chain reaction.

EMILE BERLINER (1851–1929): INVENTOR OF THE GRAMOPHONE

Emile Berliner was born in Hanover, Germany, in 1851. He immigrated to the United States in 1870, where the developments of the era excited both his interest in science and his ambitions as an inventor.

In 1876, Berliner witnessed a demonstration of Alexander Graham Bell's new telephone in Washington, D.C. Berliner realized that one of the instrument's weaknesses was its transmitter. Berliner built a new transmitter—a sort of microphone—that increased the volume of the transmitted voice and made it more audible.

After several years spent improving Bell's telephone, Berliner began working, in 1886, on the invention that was to prove his most important contribution. The gramophone, as he called it, was a means of recording and reproducing sound. He patented this invention, which first used cylinders and then switched to disc records for the recordings, in 1887.

CHAPTER 4

Energy Changers

As we have already seen, energy can change from one form to another. When you flip a light switch, electrical energy is changed into light and heat energy by the light bulb. This is called energy conversion. You can usually follow the "energy chain," the trail that energy takes as it changes from one form into another.

Think about the energy chain of an apple. It starts with sunlight energy striking the leaves of the apple tree and making food for the tree and the fruit to grow. Some of that energy is stored as chemical energy inside the apple. When you eat an apple you are transferring the chemical energy into your body. You will use this energy to move, talk, and keep warm. Can you follow the energy chains of these energy changes?

- the egg you boiled on the stove
- the electric fan you used to keep cool
- the bicycle you rode over to your friend's house
- the bus you took to school

An apple is a food store. It contains substances, such as sugar, that are rich in chemical energy that came from sunlight. When you eat the apple, you change the apple's stored energy into your own!

When you take a bus, the bus is changing chemical energy stored in its fuel into other sorts of energy in order to get you to school.

Scientists have studied many energy chains like these. They have discovered that whenever energy moves from one point to another in one of these chains, the energy is likely to change into several different forms along the way. Even with all these changes, the total amount of energy they can measure always stays the same. They proved that energy cannot be created or destroyed as it changes forms. In scientific terms, this is called the **law of conservation of energy**. Conservation means "keeping the same," and it tells you that energy isn't made or lost anywhere along the energy chain.

Everything in the universe is part of an energy chain. Although we sometimes say we "use up" a lot of energy, we do not, in fact, ever use it up. We simply pass it on, or change it into different forms.

SEA OF ENERGY

"Our universe is a sea of energy—free, clean energy. It is all out there waiting, for us to set sail upon it."

Robert Adams, New Zealand scientist who specialized in research into alternative forms of energy, 1920–2006

Transfer of Energy

Machines

A machine is an energy changer. A machine can be defined as any object that we can use to make a task easier to do. So a screwdriver is a machine just as much as an earthmover or a computer is a machine.

Machines can magnify force, or they can magnify movement. An example of a force magnifier is a pair of pliers. Imagine trying to twist two metal wires together using just your fingers. It wouldn't be easy. By squeezing the handles of the pliers, however, the force is concentrated between the jaws of the pliers on a small area of the wires.

A hand drill is a movement magnifier. When you turn the handle, the drill itself turns much faster. It has a cog—a wheel with teeth—that connects with another cog to transfer the movement from the slow-moving handle to the faster-turning drill.

A wheelbarrow is a type of lever. The wheel acts as a fulcrum so that you can raise a load when you use effort to lift the handles.

Pliers also are an example of a simple sort of machine called a **lever**. Levers help us move heavy loads as well as exert much force without much effort. The lever idea is used to make a wheelbarrow easy to push, to take the top off a bottle, and to cut paper with scissors.

An earthmover uses powerful levers to raise and lower its long arm and also to scoop up a heavy load.

Did You Know?

Levers have been used for centuries. By 1550 B.C., they were used in Egypt and India to move heavy objects in building work.

JAMES PRESCOTT JOULE (1818–1889): PHYSICIST AND ENGINEER

James Prescott Joule was born in 1818 near Manchester, England. Joule experimented with the relationship between energy and work (work in the scientific sense, meaning the relationship between the amount of force needed to move something and the distance that it is moved). His research was so important that the international unit of energy, the joule, was named in his honor.

Much of Joule's research focused on heat energy. He discovered that a certain, measured amount of work always generates the same amount of heat. In one of his experiments, Joule measured the heat generated by turning a paddle wheel inside a container of water. From this experiment, he discovered that a set amount of work always resulted in the same rise in water temperature.

Joule's work contributed to the law of the conservation of energy, which states that energy is not created or destroyed but, rather, is simply changed from one form to another.

Sources of Energy

Our towns and cities need a huge amount of energy—usually in the form of electricity—to run homes, schools, offices, factories, shopping malls, transportation systems, and more. A lot of this energy comes from burning what are called fossil fuels—coal, oil, and natural gas—in power plants.

ELECTRIC ENERGY

"Electric power is everywhere present in unlimited quantities and can drive the world's machinery without the need of coal, oil, gas, or any other of the common fuels."

Nikola Tesla, Serbian-American inventor and scientist, 1856–1943

Oil is a valuable fossil fuel on which most of us depend for our energy needs.

Fossil Fuels

Coal was formed as the remains of ancient trees and other vegetation decayed and became buried in mud. After millions of years of heat and the weight of the layers above them, those remains turned into the type of rock we call coal. Oil and gas are chemicals made as the decayed bodies of small plants and animals were heated and squeezed by layers of sand that turned to rock beneath the ocean floor.

Earth has only limited supplies of coal, oil, and natural gas, or fossil fuels as they are called. They are a nonrenewable energy source. The term *nonrenewable* means that when this source is gone, there is no way to replace, or renew, it. Current estimates of world oil and natural gas reserves and predictions for their consumption suggest these fuels will run out around 2040 or

2050. Coal stocks are predicted to last longer, perhaps three hundred years.

Using fossil fuels brings a number of dangers, particularly to the environment. The evidence is becoming stronger all the time that the waste carbon dioxide gas, produced when fossil fuels burn, is making the average temperature of our planet rise.

Carbon dioxide is called a greenhouse gas because it traps the Sun's infrared heat radiation in the atmosphere, like the glass in a greenhouse, so that it can't radiate out into space. This adds to the effect called global warming. Global warming is already causing

Our "24-hours-a-day" cities use up vast amounts of electricity. How different would your life be without it?

dramatic changes to the weather in many parts of the world, including more floods, droughts, and hurricanes than usual.

Alternatives to Fossil Fuels— Nuclear Power

Nuclear power is generated by bombarding the nucleus of an atom with neutron particles. When this happens, huge amounts of heat are produced. The heat is used to boil water, turning it into steam. The steam turns turbine blades that are linked to electricity generators.

Nuclear power stations do not produce polluting gases, but they are very expensive to build and to close down at the end of their working lives. The buildings and interior machinery become radioactive over the course of their operation. Radioactive waste from nuclear power plants remains dangerous for thousands of years. Scientists, engineers, and geologists are working to find environmentally safe ways to dispose of hazardous radioactive waste. Solutions include turning the waste into a substance like glass and burying it deep underground, storing it on the deep ocean floor, or even firing it into space in a rocket! Wherever it is placed, it remains dangerously radioactive.

Water Power

The energy in moving water has been used throughout history to power waterwheels and the machinery that can be driven by

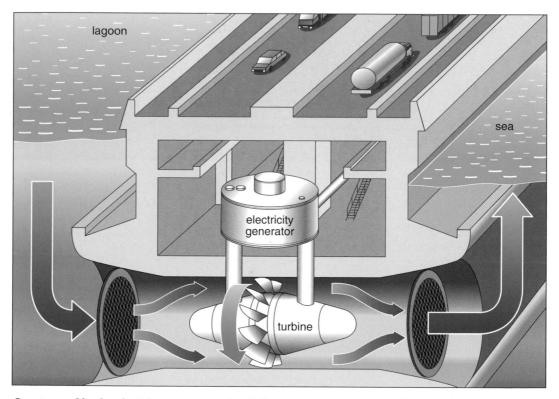

One type of hydroelectric power uses the daily movement of ocean tides. At low tide, water in the **lagoon** is allowed to run out toward the sea over a turbine. As the water turns the turbine blades, the generator makes electricity. At high tide, sea water flows back into the lagoon to start the process again.

POOR ENERGY

"The energy produced by the breaking down of the atom is a very poor kind of thing. Anyone who expects a source of power from the transformation of these atoms is talking moonshine."

Ernest Rutherford, New Zealand atomic scientist, 1871–1937

them, such as mills for grinding corn and looms for weaving cloth.

Dams are used to capture energy from water. Water held back by a dam is a source of potential energy. When the water is released and flows through the dam, its gravitational potential energy is turned into kinetic energy. This energy is used to turn the blades of turbines that generate electricity. Energy produced from the movement of water is called hydroelectric energy.

Wind Power

For centuries, people have also used the energy in the wind to do helpful work. Wind energy has been used for everything from powering sailing ships to grinding corn in windmills.

Today, we build wind turbines that can harness the energy in moving air—which is what wind is—to generate electricity for single homes or for whole communities. The turbine towers can be very tall. Some stand around 200 feet (60 m) high—with blades up to 165 feet (50 m) long—so that they can capture as much of the wind as possible.

Wind turbines make best use of the wind when there are many of them together in one place. Some wind farms contain several hundred turbines. People have different opinions about whether it is a good thing to build wind farms in the countryside because windy places are often beautiful. Wind turbines can spoil that beauty.

Power from Sunlight

The Sun is an important energy source that won't run out for a *very* long time and doesn't pollute the environment. The Sun's energy can be changed into electricity by using solar cells.

ENERGY FROM SUNBEAMS

"I have no doubt that we will be successful in harnessing the sun's energy. . . . If sunbeams were weapons of war, we would have had solar energy centuries ago."

Sir George Porter, British physical chemist, 1920–2002

Transfer of Energy

Many homes, offices, and even schools are now being built with solar panels, such as the ones on these roofs, to trap sunlight energy and use it to generate electricity.

Solar cells are made like a sandwich, with two layers of the element silicon treated with other chemicals and stuck together. When sunlight shines on these layers, a tiny electric current flows between them. Thousands of these cells together can generate a significant amount of electricity. You can find solar cells powering many things, from calculators to outdoor lamps and space satellites.

Power from Hot Rocks

Below Earth's surface is a huge storehouse of heat energy, called geothermal energy.

Some rocks in the Earth's crust are at temperatures of almost 1,800 °F (1,000 °C).

Much of this energy stays below the Earth's surface. Some of this energy comes to the surface as natural hot water springs or geysers. When the temperature of these porous hot rocks rises above 220 °F (104 °C), they hold enough heat energy to turn cold water, when it is piped down into the rocks, to steam. This steam can then turn a turbine and generate electricity.

By 2006, twenty-four countries, including the United States, were using geothermal energy to produce some of their electricity.

Did You Know?

A pinhead-size piece of uranium nuclear fuel contains as much energy as nearly 530 gallons (2,000 liters) of oil.

These pipes carry steam made using heat from hot rocks below Earth's surface. The steam turns a steam turbine to generate electricity that is carried by power lines to local communities.

GERALD PEARSON (1905–1987), CALVIN FULLER (1902–1994), AND DARYL CHAPIN (1906–1995): INVENTORS OF THE SILICON SOLAR CELL

In 1954, American researchers Gerald Pearson, Calvin Fuller, and Daryl Chapin, working at Bell Laboratories, New York City, designed and built a silicon solar cell. This solar cell was capable of converting 6 percent of the Sun's light energy that arrives at the Earth's surface into an electric current.

The inventors exposed strips of the element silicon to sunlight and connected them to sensitive electronics, which they found they could generate an electric current. They had made the forerunner to the solar panel.

CHAPTER 6

Energy in Living Things

Without sunshine, Earth would have no life. The Sun's energy drives a natural system that takes substances out of the air and the soil and uses them over and over again to build the bodies of all living things.

Even the largest trees on Earth—the giant redwoods of California—are made up of atoms taken from the air and the soil. It is in the leaves of the trees that the atoms are brought together in a series of chemical reactions to produce the materials that will become new redwood cells. But, as with all living things, the tree will eventually die and

Giant redwoods are huge chemical factories, changing light energy from the Sun, our nearest star, into food energy stored in the leaves and trunk of the tree.

decay, so that its atoms will return to the air and the soil . . . ready to be used again by another plant!

Photosynthesis: Food from Light!

The food-making process that goes on in plants is called **photosynthesis**, which means "using light to make new substances." Using energy from sunlight, plants turn carbon dioxide gas, which they take in through their leaves, and water, which they absorb through their roots, into a type of sugar called glucose. The glucose is then the raw material for a whole factory of reactions that make food for the plant.

Below are two equations—one using words and the other using scientific symbols—to describe this process. The arrows that connect the names of the raw materials to the names of the final products mean "are combined together chemically to make..." something.

water + carbon dioxide $\rightarrow$ glucose + oxygen

$$6\,H_2O + 6\,CO_2 \rightarrow C_6H_{12}O_6 + 6\,O_2$$

Leaves are important to the food-making process because that's where most of the green pigment, called chlorophyll, is stored.

(That explains why leaves are usually green, too.) The chlorophyll absorbs the Sun's light energy and converts it into stored chemical energy in glucose molecules.

Glucose is also the starting point for producing other substances that the plant stores. These substances include starch and oil in stems, roots, fruits, and seeds; and proteins in seeds and nuts. People use many of these plant parts as either food or other products.

Food Chains

Leaves grow on a lettuce plant, snails feed on the leaves, and birds eat the snails. Along with the food, the snails get energy that was stored in the lettuce leaves, and the birds get energy that was stored in the snails, including energy that came from the lettuce—which got its energy from a star, the Sun. This movement of food energy from one living thing to another is called a food chain. We can show this chain with words connected by arrows that point in the direction that the food energy travels.

lettuce → snail → bird

Every food chain starts with a **producer**—an organism that can make its own food. In land-based food chains, the producers are plants of all sizes. In the oceans, the producers are microscopic plants called phytoplankton.

Animals are **consumers**, which means that they get their food by eating plants or other animals. Consumers that eat only plants, such as deer and snails, are called herbivores. Consumers that eat only other animals, such as hawks and spiders, are called carnivores. Those that eat both plants and animals are called omnivores.

plant → herbivore → carnivore or omnivore

Food chains may be as short as two links. Some may have five or even six links, or more, but that is unusual. Most consist of only a few links. After two or three types of animals have passed the food energy to the

This simple food chain has four links. The flowers are eaten by beetles, which are eaten by rats, which are eaten by owls. In this way, energy is passed through the food chain from the flowers (the producer) to each of the animals (the consumers).

next one, the chain reaches the animal called the top consumer. The top consumer is not usually hunted by other animals. That is, it has no predators.

Food energy is lost between each link in the chain. As animals run around, some of their energy is lost as heat. Still more is lost when animals die instead of being eaten by the next animal in the chain.

Food Webs

Plants are usually eaten by more than one sort of animal, and most herbivores eat several kinds of plants. Many carnivores also hunt different species of herbivores. An omnivore may eat a certain type of plant, and it may also eat an animal that eats the same type of plant. This means most living things are in more than one food chain. In a community of many plants and animals living together, the food chains interlink in a complicated way, called a food web.

It is important to study food chains and webs for many reasons. One of these is to understand why we need to conserve **biodiversity**. Another is to be able to predict the effects of **pollution** and other human impact on the other living things in the environment.

Conserving Biodiversity

Biodiversity is the number of different species of animals and plants that live in a given community, such as a wood or a pond. This community is called a habitat.

If you could count the number of plants and animals in a habitat, you would find that a lot of plants feed a smaller number of herbivores. These herbivores, in turn, feed an even smaller number of carnivores who are prey for the one or two top consumers. This is called an energy pyramid. The energy pyramid shows how energy is lost at each step along a food chain.

We need to be concerned about keeping each habitat's energy pyramid healthy and working. If, for example, something kills half of the plants in the habitat, then that could mean that only half the herbivores and half the carnivores survive as well. It could even mean that the top consumers or an entire species might die out all together, which would mean less biodiversity.

EUGENE ODUM (1913–2002): ECOLOGIST

Eugene Odum was born in North Carolina and graduated from the University of Illinois. He was one of the first scientists to use the word ecosystem to describe the relationships between living things and their environment.

Odum wrote a pioneering book on ecology with his brother Howard, also an ecologist, called *Fundamentals of Ecology*. The book came out in 1953 and influenced an entire generation of ecologists, so much so that Eugene Odum is often called the "father of modern ecology."

Predicting the Effects of Pollution

Once scientists figure out a habitat's food web, they can see the links between each of the living things in that web. This means, for example, that if a pollutant got into a habitat—such as a pesticide in a river—and started killing plants or animals, the scientists could tell which plants and animals were most at risk. The scientists might decide the endangered species needed to be caught and moved out while the river was being cleaned.

Clean energy, such as energy from biofuels, hydrogen, wind, and the Sun, may help living things in all of Earth's food webs have healthier lives in the future.

Canola, a vegetable oil, is now being grown to make biodiesel—an alternative to gasoline. It burns much more cleanly than gasoline and traditional diesel. About 800 acres of canola can produce 63,400 gallons (240,000 liters) of biodiesel.

BIOFUEL

Biofuel is any fuel that comes from recently living organisms or their waste products. In the United States, corn and soybeans are grown especially for use as biofuels. Waste from industry, agriculture, and households can also be used to produce energy. Examples of the products that can be used to generate energy include straw, manure, sewage, garbage, and food leftovers.

One advantage of biofuels, when compared with most other fuels, is that the energy inside the fuel can be stored for a long time and without any danger to the environment. That is, if it's spilled, it doesn't pose any threat to the environment because it is not poisonous, and it is biodegradeable, so it will decay naturally.

Since the carbon in biofuels was originally taken from carbon dioxide in the atmosphere by plants, burning it does not result in an overall increase of carbon dioxide in Earth's atmosphere. As a result, many people see biofuels as a way to replace nonrenewable sources of energy, like fossil fuels, and reduce the amount of carbon dioxide put into the atmosphere.

atom the smallest possible part of a pure chemical element, such as gold or hydrogen, that has the chemical properties of the element

battery a device that stores electrical energy and can release it when the battery is part of a circuit

biodiversity the number of different species of animals and plants that live in a given environment

chain reaction a series of connected events or actions, each put into motion by the one before it

chemical energy the energy stored in the bonds between atoms in a molecule and released by means of chemical reactions

conduction the transfer of heat energy through a substance when atoms and molecules in the substance collide and transfer energy from one to another

consumer any living organism that eats, or consumes, food to keep it alive

convection the transfer of heat energy through a gas or a liquid by circulating currents of air or water

electrical energy energy made available when an electric charge flows through a substance that can conduct electricity

electromagnetic radiation waves with both electrical and magnetic properties and moving with the speed of light. Includes gamma radiation; X-rays, ultraviolet, visible, and infrared radiation; and radio waves

electromagnetic spectrum the complete range of electromagnetic radiation— waves of electromagnetic energy— arranged in order from the longest to the shortest

energy the capacity of a body or system to do work

Gulf Stream a warm-water ocean current flowing from the Gulf of Mexico north along the U.S. coast into the North Atlantic. This convection current results from the sun-warmed water of the equator region of Earth moving north and south toward colder water

interference the interaction caused by the intersection of two waves

kinetic energy the energy of any object that is moving; also known as movement energy

lagoon an area of water separated from the sea by a reef or barrier

law of the conservation of energy a principle stating that energy can't be created or destroyed, but it can change its form

lens a piece of transparent material used to make light rays converge (bend inward) or diverge (bend outward) to make images

lever a rigid bar that tilts on a fulcrum (pivot point)

light energy electromagnetic radiation that can be detected by the human eye

machines devices that make it easier for people to do work, such as levers, automobiles, or jackhammers

magma the molten material flowing deep within the Earth

mantle the layer of Earth below its crust and above its core. Earth's mantle is estimated to be 1,800 miles (2,900 km) thick.

microbes microscopic organisms, some of which are germs

mirror a polished, shiny surface that forms images by reflecting light

molecule the smallest particle in a chemical compound, for example, sodium chloride, that has the chemical properties of that compound

nuclear energy the energy stored in the nucleus of an atom, which can be released during a chain reaction, such as fission

opaque does not allow light to pass through

photosynthesis the process that takes place inside green plants and certain other organisms to make carbohydrates (such as glucose) from carbon dioxide and water, using light as the energy source

pollution unwanted substances contaminating the environment, either intentionally or accidentally

potential energy energy stored within an object because of its position, what it contains, or what has been done to it

producer a plant that makes its own food by photosynthesis and is at the beginning of a food chain

reflection the bouncing of light off a polished surface, such as a mirror, to create an an image of an object

radiation heat and light energy given out from a source such as the Sun

refraction the bending of light rays as they enter or leave a transparent material, such as when light passes through a glass of water

sound energy the energy that travels through a material as a wave when an object vibrates, for example, when a guitar string is plucked

temperature a property of matter that measures how much movement energy its particles have. There are several scales used to measure temperature, e.g., Kelvin, Celsius, Fahrenheit.

translucent allowing light to shine through, but not transparent enough to see through clearly

transmission when light waves or other energy waves hit a material and continue on through

transmitter a device that carries signals to your radio or television

transparent clear enough not to block light; can be seen through

Books

Hayhurst, Chris.
*Biofuel of the Future: New Ways of
Turning Organic Matter into Energy.*
Library of Future Energy (series).
Rosen Publishing Group, 2003

Hayhurst, Chris.
*Hydrogen Power: New Ways of
Turning Fuel Cells into Energy.*
Library of Future Energy (series).
Rosen Publishing Group, 2003

Jones, Susan.
*Solar Power of the Future: New Ways
of Turning Sunlight into Energy.*
Library of Future Energy (series).
Rosen Publishing Group, 2003

Sherman, Josepha.
Geothermal Power.
Energy at Work (series).
Capstone Press, 2006

Tecco, Betsy Dru Dru.
*Wind Power of the Future:
New Ways of Wind into Energy.*
Library of Future Energy (series).
Rosen Publishing Group, 2003

Various.
Nuclear Energy.
(Discovery Channel School Science).
Gareth Stevens, 2002

Web Sites

U.S. Department of Energy
Teacher and student pages on energy
resources and activities.
www.energy.gov

**EIA: Energy Information
Administration**
Background information on U.S. energy
resources, including data.
www.eia.doe.gov/emeu/aer/eh/frame.html

Environmental Protection Agency
Energy information and links related to
energy conservation and pollution control.
www.epa.gov/ebtpages/pollenergy.html

Food Chains and Food Webs
Information and activities about food chains
and webs.
ecokids.earthday.ca/pub/eco_info/topics/
frogs/chain_reaction/index.cfm

Light
Background information on the properties
of light, reflection, refraction, and some uses
of mirrors and lenses.
www.opticalres.com/kidoptx.html

Web Sites (cont.)

Machines

Information and activities to explore what machines can do.
www.edheads.org/activities/
simple-machines/index.htm

Explanations of how the so-called six simple machines work.
www.coe.uh.edu/archive/science/
science_lessons/scienceles1/finalhome.htm

Publisher's note to educators and parents: Our editors have carefully reviewed these Web sites to ensure that they are suitable for children. Many Web sites change frequently, however, and we cannot guarantee that a site's future contents will continue to meet our high standards of quality and educational value. Be advised that children should be closely supervised whenever they access the Internet.